New Careers for the
21st Century:
Finding Your Role in
the Global Renewal

# MODERN MECHANICS:

## *MAINTAINING TOMORROW'S GREEN VEHICLES*

# New Careers for the 21st Century: Finding Your Role in the Global Renewal

**CAREERS IN GREEN ENERGY:**
*FUELING THE WORLD WITH RENEWABLE RESOURCES*

**ENVIRONMENTAL SCIENCE & PROTECTION:**
*KEEPING OUR PLANET GREEN*

**FREELANCE AND TECHNICAL WRITERS:**
*WORDS FOR SALE*

**GREEN CONSTRUCTION:**
*CREATING ENERGY-EFFICIENT, LOW-IMPACT BUILDINGS*

**MEDIA IN THE 21ST CENTURY:**
*ARTISTS, ANIMATORS, AND GRAPHIC DESIGNERS*

**MEDICAL TECHNICIANS:**
*HEALTH-CARE SUPPORT FOR THE 21ST CENTURY*

**MODERN MECHANICS:**
*MAINTAINING TOMORROW'S GREEN VEHICLES*

**THE PHARMACEUTICAL INDUSTRY:**
*BETTER MEDICINE FOR THE 21ST CENTURY*

**PHYSICIANS' ASSISTANTS & NURSES:**
*NEW OPPORTUNITIES IN THE 21ST-CENTURY HEALTH SYSTEM*

**SOCIAL WORKERS:** *FINDING SOLUTIONS FOR TOMORROW'S SOCIETY*

**TOMORROW'S ENTERPRISING SCIENTISTS:**
*COMPUTER SOFTWARE DESIGNERS AND SPECIALISTS*

**TOMORROW'S TEACHERS:**
*URBAN LEADERSHIP, EMPOWERING STUDENTS & IMPROVING LIVES*

**TOMORROW'S TRANSPORTATION:**
*GREEN SOLUTIONS FOR AIR, LAND, & SEA*

**21ST-CENTURY COUNSELORS:**
*NEW APPROACHES TO MENTAL HEALTH & SUBSTANCE ABUSE*

**THERAPY JOBS IN EDUCATIONAL SETTINGS:**
*SPEECH, PHYSICAL, OCCUPATIONAL & AUDIOLOGY*

New Careers for the 21st Century: Finding Your Role in the Global Renewal

# MODERN MECHANICS:
## MAINTAINING TOMORROW'S GREEN VEHICLES

by Malinda Miller

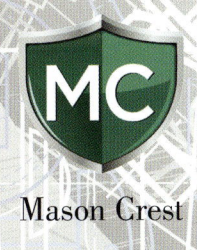

Mason Crest

EAST CHICAGO PUBLIC LIBRARY
EAST CHICAGO, INDIANA

MODERN MECHANICS:

*MAINTAINING TOMORROW'S GREEN VEHICLES*

Copyright © 2011 by Mason Crest, an imprint of National Highlights, Inc. All rights reserved. No part of this publication may be reproduced or transmitted in any form or by any means, electronic or mechanical, including photocopying, recording, taping, or any information storage and retrieval system, without permission from the publisher.

MASON CREST
450 Parkway Drive, Suite D
Broomall, Pennsylvania 19008
(866) MCP-BOOK (toll free)
www.masoncrest.com

9 8 7 6 5 4 3 2

Library of Congress Cataloging-in-Publication Data

Miller, Malinda, 1979–
  Modern mechanics : maintaining tomorrow's green vehicles / by Malinda Miller.
      p. cm. — (New careers for the 21st century)
  Includes bibliographical references and index.
    ISBN 978-1-4222-1818-1         ISBN 978-1-4222-1811-2 (series)
    ISBN 978-1-4222-2039-9 (ppb)   ISBN 978-1-4222-2032-0 (series ppb)
  1. Machinery—Maintenance and repair—Vocational guidance. 2. Mechanics (Persons)—Vocational guidance.  I. Title.
  TJ157.M55 2011
  629.28'7023—dc22
                            2010016870

Produced by Harding House Publishing Service, Inc.
www.hardinghousepages.com
Interior design by MK Bassett-Harvey.
Cover design by Torque Advertising + Design.
Printed in USA by Bang Printing.

# CONTENTS

Introduction...6

Chapter 1:
What Do Mechanics Do?...9

Chapter 2:
Green Vehicles...23

Chapter 3:
Education and Training...37

Chapter 4:
Job Opportunities and Related Occupations...47

Chapter 5:
The Future of Mechanics...55

Further Reading...60

Find Out More on the Internet...61

Bibliography...62

Index...62

Picture Credits...63

About the Author/About the Consultant...64

# INTRODUCTION

Be careful as you begin to plan your career.

To get yourself in the best position to begin the career of your dreams, you need to know what the "green world" will look like and what jobs will be created and what jobs will become obsolete. Just think, according to the Bureau of Labor Statistics, the following jobs are expected to severely decline by 2012:

- word processors and data-entry keyers
- stock clerks and order fillers
- secretaries
- electrical and electronic equipment assemblers
- computer operators
- telephone operators
- postal service mail sorters and processing-machine operators
- travel agents

These are just a few of the positions that will decrease or become obsolete as we move forward into the century.

You need to know what the future jobs will be. How do you find them? One way is to look where money is being invested. Many firms and corporations are now making investments in startup and research enterprises. These companies may become the "Microsoft" and "Apple" of the twenty-first century. Look at what is being researched and what technology is needed to obtain the results.

# INTRODUCTION

Green world, green economy, green technology—they all say the same things: the way we do business today is changing. Every industry will be shaped by the world's new focus on creating a sustainable lifestyle, one that won't deplete our natural and economic resources.

The possibilities are unlimited. Almost any area that will conserve energy and reduce the dependency on fossil fuels is open to new and exciting career paths. Many of these positions have not even been identified yet and will only come to light as the technology progresses and new discoveries are made in the way we use that technology. And the best part about this is that our government is behind us. The U.S. government wants to help you get the education and training you'll need to succeed and grow in this new and changing economy. The U.S. Department of Labor has launched a series of initiatives to support and promote green job creation. To view the report, visit: www.dol.gov/dol/green/earthday_reportA.pdf.

The time to decide on your future is now. This series, NEW CAREERS FOR THE 21ST CENTURY: FINDING YOUR ROLE IN THE GLOBAL RENEWAL, can act as the first step toward your continued education, training, and career path decisions. Take the first steps that will lead you—and the planet—to a productive and sustainable future.

Mike Puglisi
Department of Labor, District I Director (New York/New Jersey)
IAWP (International Association of Workforce Professionals)

> You must be the change you wish to see in the world.
>
> —Mahatma Gandhi

### ABOUT THE QUOTE

The time has come to change the way we live, for the sake of our planet, for the sake of future generations, and for the sake of our own lives and well-being. You can talk about how things ought to change—or you can be a part of the change. The job you choose to do in life is one of your most powerful tools for bringing about change in the world around you. If you choose a career working on green vehicles, you will be contributing to a new and better world for us all.

# CHAPTER 1
# WHAT DO MECHANICS DO?

## WORDS TO KNOW

*mechanical*: Related to machines or machinery.

*sophisticated*: Complex and intricate.

*components*: Parts, especially of a machine.

*diagnostic*: Dealing with the diagnosis of illness or problems—in other words, figuring out what's wrong.

*digital*: Information written in a numerical code to be used by computers or other electronic equipment.

*repair service estimator*: A person who tests and inspects a machine and then gives an estimate for any work needed and what that work would likely cost.

*service advisor*: a person who works with customers to figure out what repairs or maintenance their vehicle needs.

*pneumatic*: Containing or run by air or gas under pressure.

*lathes*: Machines with a rotating part that turn a piece of metal or wood against a changeable cutting tool.

*global positioning system*: A navigational system that uses signals from orbiting satellites to locate a position on Earth; commonly called GPS.

*refrigerants*: Substances that cause cooling.

Ask any car owner and he will tell you how important it is to have an auto mechanic who is talented, reasonably priced, and trustworthy. This is especially true in suburban and rural areas with little or no public transportation. In many metropolitan areas, public transit offers an option for getting from place to place, but in areas with no subway, buses, or trains, people depend on their cars to get them—well, everywhere. And if a person's car breaks down, she will want to get it fixed as quickly as possible so she can get back to her normal routine.

In addition to the widespread need for mechanics, there is a growing need for mechanics that know how to work on the new generation of "green" vehicles. Cars today already have different maintenance needs than the cars of the past, since more and more are dependent on computers for their operation. The hybrid, electric, or other alternative fuel cars on the roads today have additional maintenance requirements that are different than gasoline-powered cars.

## Choosing the Right Career

The young adults of today will be the job force of tomorrow, so choosing a career that will best fit with the needs of the changing world will be important to job satisfaction and a successful life. With the vast array of career and job options, young adults need to understand which work will be the best match for their interests, talents, goals, and personality types. If you like working with your hands and solving problems, a career as a mechanic might be right for you.

## It's Not Just Cars

The word "mechanic" for most people means a person who fixes cars, but there are many other types of mechanics. A mechanic is any worker who repairs machinery. Besides auto mechanics, this includes:

air conditioning and refrigerator mechanics
aircraft mechanics
bicycle mechanics
boiler mechanics
diesel mechanics
general mechanics
millwrights
motorcycle mechanics
tank mechanics

Certain job industries are expected to gain importance within the early decades of the twenty-first century. In general, the opportunities for automotive service technicians and mechanics are actually expected to increase at a slower than average rate. According to the United States Bureau of Labor Statistics, the number of jobs across all industries is expected to increase by 14 percent through the year 2020, while the number of jobs for mechanics is expected to increase by only 5 percent. However, job opportunities are expected to be very good for the mechanics that complete a training program and receive special certification.

## Automotive Service Technicians and Mechanics

Automotive service technicians and mechanics inspect cars, perform basic care maintenance, diagnose complex problems, and repair cars and small trucks that run on gasoline, electricity, or alternative fuels. The tasks and responsibilities of modern mechanics are different from the mechanics of the past, as they have shifted from simple *mechanical* repairs to more *sophisticated* technological work. Vehicles today rely more on electronic systems and computers for operation. This increase in the technology of cars and trucks requires mechanics who have an understanding of how these complex parts work together to run the vehicles. They must also be able to work with computerized shop equipment, electronic *components* and *diagnostic* equipment, *digital* manuals and reference materials, while still keeping the ability to work with their hands and hand tools on the mechanical parts of the vehicles.

When mechanical or electrical troubles occur in a vehicle, mechanics start their investigation by getting a description of the problem from the owner or from the *repair service estimator* or *service advisor* who spoke to the owner. To find the problem, mechanics first test to see whether all components and systems

CHAPTER 1: WHAT DO MECHANICS DO?

*Mechanics of today need to be able to move back and forth between traditional mechanical work on parts like the engine, and more technological work involving the modern electronic and computerized components.*

are secure and working properly. Then, they locate the specific parts or systems that might be the cause of the problem. For example, if an air conditioner malfunctions, the mechanic would first check for a simple problem, such as a low coolant level. She would then move on to more complex possibilities, such as a bad drive-train connection that has shorted out the air conditioner.

As part of their investigation, technicians test drive the vehicle or use testing equipment, including onboard and handheld diagnostic computers or compression gauges. Besides helping to locate the problem, these tests help determine if the problem is fixable or if a new part is needed. Speed and correct diagnosis are important because parts are expensive and faster repairs allow shops to accept more business.

During normal inspections, mechanics test and care for engines and other major vehicle components. Sometimes mechanics repair or replace worn parts before they cause breakdowns or damage the vehicle. Technicians usually follow a checklist to ensure that they examine every critical part. Belts, hoses, plugs, brakes, fuel systems, and other potentially troublesome items are watched closely.

## Tools

Automotive service technicians use a variety of tools in their work. They use power tools, such as *pneumatic* wrenches, to remove bolts quickly; machine tools like *lathes* and grinding machines to rebuild brakes; welding and flame-cutting equipment to remove and repair exhaust systems; and jacks and hoists to lift cars and

CHAPTER 1: WHAT DO MECHANICS DO?

*A car is a complicated piece of machinery, with many different interrelated parts. Understanding how a car works is a basic part of being a good mechanic.*

engines. They also use more familiar hand tools, such as screwdrivers, pliers, and wrenches, to work on small parts and in hard-to-reach places. Mechanics usually provide their own hand tools, and experienced workers often have thousands of dollars invested in them. Employers furnish the larger and more expensive power tools, such as engine analyzers and other diagnostic equipment.

Modern repair shops also use a lot of computers for various tasks. Car manufacturers provide standards for every car. Mechanics compare readouts from computerized diagnostic testing devices to these acceptable standards to help diagnose possible problems. Readings that stray from acceptable levels guide the mechanic to the part of the vehicle that needs to be more

MODERN MECHANICS: *MAINTAINING TOMORROW'S GREEN VEHICLES*

*Car mechanics need to learn how to use many different types of tools. These mechanics are using a torch to weld part of the exhaust system.*

closely inspected. Shops can receive technical manual updates from manufacturers through the Internet, or through the purchase of software packages. In addition, manufacturers supply service information, technical service bulletins, and other databases that allow mechanics to keep up with common problems and learn new procedures.

Computers are also used extensively as part of modern vehicles to run components from the engine to the radio. In fact, most modern automotive systems, such as the braking, transmission, and steering systems, are controlled primarily by computers and electronic components. Additionally, high-end vehicles often have *global positioning systems* (GPS), accident-avoidance systems, and other new computer-based features with which technicians will need to become familiar. As a result, shops need more and more high-tech tools to allow for diagnosis and repair of this computer equipment. Finally, as more alternate-fuel vehicles are purchased, more automotive service technicians will need to learn the science behind these automobiles and how to repair them.

## Specializations

Automotive service technicians in large shops often specialize in certain types of repairs.

## Air-Conditioning Technicians

Automotive air-conditioning repairers install and repair car air-conditioners and service their parts, such as compressors, condensers, and controls. These workers require special training in federal and state regulations governing the handling and disposal of *refrigerants*.

## Brake Mechanics

Brake repairers adjust brakes, replace brake linings and pads, and make other repairs on brake systems.

## Front-End Mechanics

Front-end mechanics align and balance wheels and repair steering mechanisms and suspension systems. They frequently use special alignment equipment and wheel-balancing machines. Some technicians specialize in both brake and front-end work.

MODERN MECHANICS: *MAINTAINING TOMORROW'S GREEN VEHICLES*

## *Transmission Technicians*

Transmission technicians and rebuilders work on gear trains, couplings, hydraulic pumps, and other parts of transmissions. In-depth knowledge of computer controls, the ability to diagnose electrical and hydraulic problems, and other specialized skills are needed to work on these complex components, which are some of the most complicated technology found in vehicles.

*Brakes, like this disc brake, are a mechanical component that need regular maintenance and often need repair.*

## Tune-Up Technicians

Tune-up technicians adjust ignition timing and valves and adjust or replace spark plugs and other parts to ensure efficient engine performance. They often use electronic testing equipment to isolate and adjust malfunctions in fuel, ignition, and emissions control systems.

## Work Environment

According to the Bureau of Labor Statistics (BLS), in 2008, most mechanics worked a standard 40-hour week, but 24 percent

*Cars are lifted into the air so that mechanics can more easily work underneath them.*

## What Kind of Person Are You?

Career-counseling experts know that certain kinds of people do best in certain kinds of jobs. John L. Holland developed the following list of personality types and the kinds of jobs that are the best match for each type. See which one (or two) are most like you. The more you understand yourself, the better you'll be able to make a good career plan for yourself.

- Realistic personality: This kind of person likes to do practical, hands-on work. He or she will most enjoy working with materials that can be touched and manipulated, such as wood, steel, tools, and machinery. This personality type enjoys jobs that require working outdoors, but he or she does NOT enjoy jobs that require a lot of paperwork or close teamwork with others.
- Investigative personality: This personality type likes to work with ideas. He or she will enjoy jobs that require lots of thinking and researching. Jobs that require mental problem solving will be a good fit for this personality.
- Artistic personality: This type of person enjoys working with forms, designs, and patterns. She or he likes jobs that require self-expression—and that don't require following a definite set of rules.
- Social personality: Jobs that require lots of teamwork with others, as well as teaching others, are a good match for this personality type. These jobs often involve helping others in some way.
- Enterprising personality: This person will enjoy planning and starting new projects, even if that involves a degree of risk-taking. He or she is good at making decisions and leading others.
- Conventional personality: An individual with this type of personality likes to follow a clear set of procedures or routines. He or she doesn't want to be the boss but prefers to work under someone else's leadership. Jobs that require working with details and facts (more than ideas) are a good fit for this personality.

worked additional hours. Some mechanics work evenings and weekends to complete jobs and satisfy customer service needs.

Usually, service technicians work indoors. Repair shops are usually well ventilated and well lighted, but some shops are drafty and noisy. Although many problems can be fixed with simple computerized adjustments, mechanics frequently work with dirty and greasy parts, in awkward positions. They often lift heavy parts and tools. As a result, minor workplace injuries are not uncommon, but technicians usually can avoid serious accidents if safety precautions are observed.

*If you see in any given situation only what everybody else can see, you can be said to be so much a representative of your culture that you are a victim of it.*

—S. I. Hayakawa

### ABOUT THE QUOTE

Learn to think outside the box. If a mechanic assumes that because engines have always run on gas, they must ALWAYS run on gas, he will never be able to adapt to a new world where cars run on clean energy. The demand for green vehicles has just begun—who knows where it will lead during your lifetime? If you want to be a modern mechanic, you must be able to be flexible, to be open to new ideas. When you approach life with that mindset, you may even come up with new ideas of your own to help change the world!

# CHAPTER 2
# GREEN VEHICLES

## Words to Know

*global warming*: The average increase in temperature of the atmosphere near the Earth's surface, which can contribute to changes in global climate patterns. Increasingly, the term climate change is preferred because it conveys that there are other changes occurring besides rising temperatures.

*ecosystems*: Places having unique physical features, encompassing air, water, and land, and including habitats that support plant and animal life.

*Industrial Revolution*: The increase in machine use and factory production that began at the end of the eighteenth century.

*emissions*: The gases and particles put into the air by a variety of sources, including factories, power plants, motor vehicles, airplanes, and natural sources such as trees and vegetation.

*ozone layer*: An upper region of the atmosphere that contains high levels of the molecule ozone, which is composed of three oxygen atoms. The ozone layer serves to absorb solar radiation, preventing it from reaching the Earth's surface.

*combustion*: The rapid combination of a fuel with oxygen, leading to the production of energy in the form of heat and light.

*particulate*: Referring to tiny particles.

*regenerative*: Having the ability to recover or restore something that has been lost.

Everything we do each day has an effect on the Earth and the natural environment. Humans alter the natural world to build homes, construct highways, and to capture water. Unfortunately, many of these activities have had negative effects on the environment and may have lasting impacts on the planet. *Global warming*, water and air pollution, and the loss of *ecosystems* are just a few of the problems facing us today. The good news is there are actions we can take to prevent further issues, and hopefully even to correct some of humans' negative effects on the planet.

## Air Pollution and Climate Change

Climate change is one of the major environmental issues facing the world today. Since the *Industrial Revolution*, human activity, such as the burning of fossil fuels, has resulted in *emissions* that absorb and emit heat, and reflect light. These emissions increase the amount of carbon dioxide (CO2) methane (CH4), nitrous oxide (N2O), and sulfur hexafluoride (SF6) in the atmosphere. These gases act like a greenhouse, trapping heat and increasing the temperature of the planet.

In addition to increasing temperatures, the changes in the atmosphere have likely caused changes in precipitation patterns, storms, and sea level. The climate and these other features of the climate can vary naturally, so determining what is due to human activity and what is natural can be challenging.

Air pollution caused by the emissions from factories and motor vehicles not only contributes to *ozone layer* damage and climate

CHAPTER 2: GREEN VEHICLES

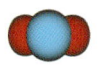

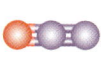

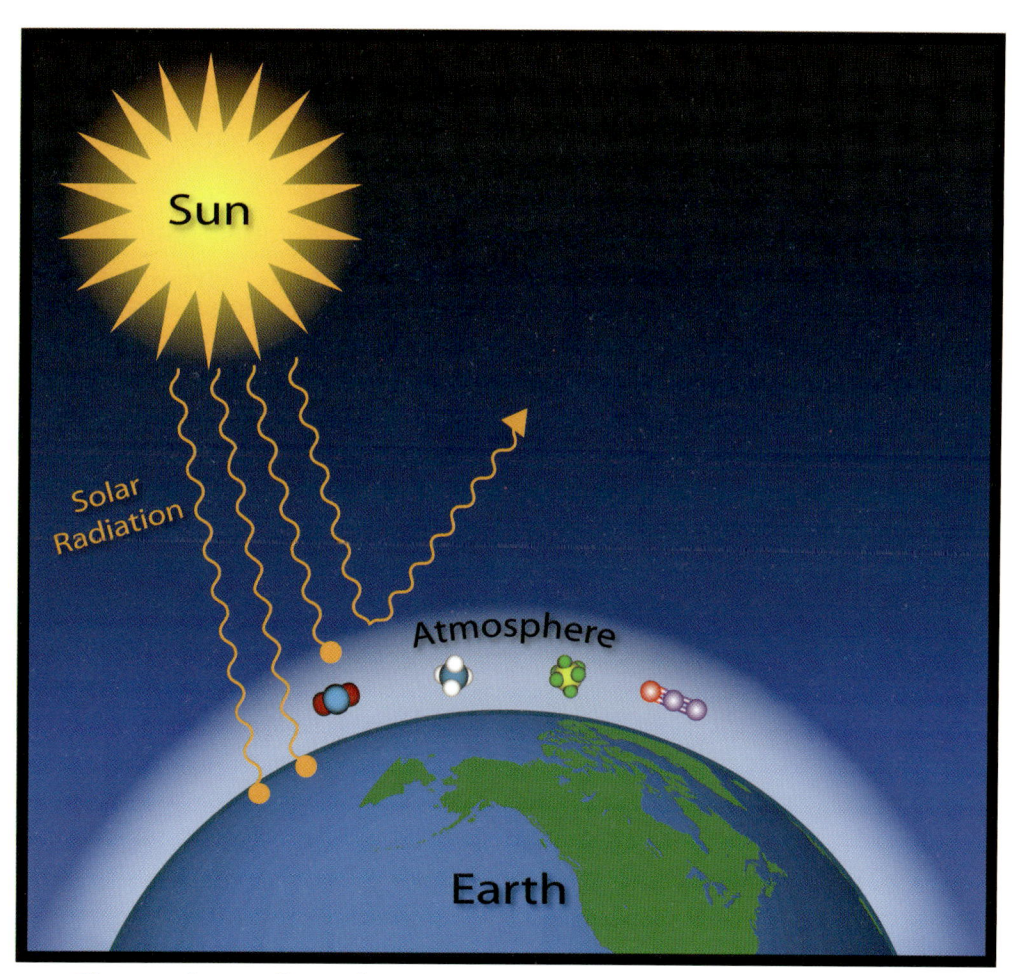

25

*The greenhouse effect is the rise in temperature that the Earth experiences because certain gases in the atmosphere trap heat from the sun. Without these gases, heat would escape back into space and Earth's average temperature would be about 60°F colder.*

change, but also affects the health of animals, plants, and entire ecosystems. Polluted air also poses a threat to human health. Poor air quality increases the occurrence of asthma. Also, the air pollution causes more damage to the ozone layer, which exposes people to more of the sun's damaging UV rays. Finally, climate change is expected to impact human health in many ways other than respiratory issues and sun exposure. The changing climate will cause health effects related to changing temperatures, of course, but it will also cause changes in weather patterns, water, air, food quality and quantity, ecosystems, agriculture, and the economy.

Many scientists focus specifically on the issues of air pollution and climate change. These scientists study the climate of the past and the present in order to better forecast the climate of the future. Predicting the future changes includes climate modeling to plan for likely impacts on ecosystems and human health. There are also numerous scientists active in the development of new ways to slow or stop climate change and its effects. Some of these scientists are developing more energy efficient, and "cleaner" cars that will not release the same amount of emissions into the atmosphere.

## Mobile Source Emissions

Cars, trucks and other transportation vehicles are considered "on-road" mobile sources of emissions and air pollution. Other "non-road" mobile sources include engines, vehicles, and other equipment used for construction, agriculture, or recreation. The

CHAPTER 2: GREEN VEHICLES 27

*There are about 251 million passenger vehicles registered in the United States alone.*

non-road category also includes airplanes, boats, and trains. Mobile sources pollute the air through **combustion** and fuel evaporation. These emissions contribute greatly to air pollution worldwide and are the primary cause of air pollution in many urban areas.

Mobile sources produce several significant air pollutants, including carbon monoxide, hydrocarbons, nitrogen oxides, and **particulate** matter. They are also a major contributor of other air poisons and greenhouse gases. Nationwide, mobile sources represent the largest contributor to toxic air pollution. Air toxics are pollutants known or suspected to cause cancer or other serious health or environmental effects.

> **Did You Know?**
> The tailpipe emissions from cars and trucks account for almost a third of the air pollution in the United States.

## Reducing Mobile Source Emissions

Since cars, trucks, and other vehicles are the source of so many different pollutants, successful pollution solutions involve a variety of approaches. From better engine design to better transit options, programs to reduce mobile source pollution must address not only vehicles, engines, and equipment, but also the fuels they use and the people who operate them. According to the United States Environmental Protection Agency (EPA), this integrated approach has already reduced emissions from individual vehicles during the past thirty years. However, since there are more cars on the road, the emissions problem is still very great. Fuels, engines, and vehicle technology will need to constantly improve to keep reducing emissions. In addition, more people will need to start choosing cleaner, alternative fuels, and driving cars with good fuel economy—in short, buying "green" vehicles.

## Green Vehicles

What makes a car "green"? Some vehicles are designed to have higher fuel economy, and to run on fuels other than petroleum-based gasoline. Green cars include hybrid cars, electric cars, hydrogen cars, biodiesel cars, and fuel cell cars. Hybrid cars are the most widely available green cars today. Most major car

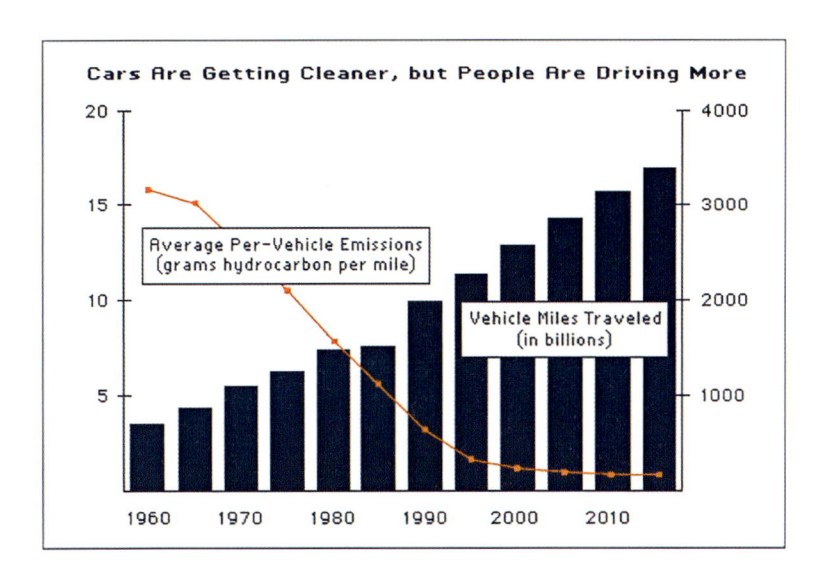

*This chart shows that modern cars are producing fewer emissions each year, but the overall emissions level is still increasing because more people own cars and drive more miles in them.*

MODERN MECHANICS: *MAINTAINING TOMORROW'S GREEN VEHICLES*

companies produce at least one hybrid option for environmentally conscious consumers.

## Hybrid Cars

A hybrid car, or a hybrid-electric vehicle, has a gasoline-fueled engine and an electric motor. The engine provides most of the power, but the electric motor helps the engine, and allows for improved fuel economy. Different levels of hybrid vehicles are available—some always need to use the engine to power the car, some are capable of driving using

> **Did You Know?**
> The Toyota Prius is the world's top selling hybrid car, with cumulative global sales of 1.6 million units by early 2010.

*The Toyota Prius was the first mass-produced hybrid vehicle. It was first released for world-wide sale in 2001.*

## How Can I Make My Car Greener?

Due to high prices, many people cannot afford to purchase a green car yet. Therefore, many people still have to buy conventional gasoline-powered cars. If this is the case, choose the most fuel-efficient car you can afford to buy and follow these simple tips to make it a "greener" car:

- Drive less: Instead of driving your car everywhere, take public transportation, carpool, ride a bike, or walk whenever possible.
- Refuel wisely: Never refill your tank beyond the automatic shut-off point, and refuel when the temperature is cooler. Both actions will reduce fuel evaporation (a factor in the production of smog).
- Maintain your vehicle properly: A car performs best (and produces lowest emissions) when it is cared for properly. Check your owner's manual for maintenance instructions.

A good mechanic can help you with this final tip. If you have a used car, and do not have the owner's manual, your mechanic can tell you the proper maintenance schedule for your vehicle. Or, if you are mechanically inclined, find the information you need to maintain the car yourself. Working on your own car will be good practice and will help familiarize you with the internal workings of an automobile. This hands-on knowledge will be helpful once you are in an automotive training program or even when you are looking for a job in the future.

# MODERN MECHANICS: *MAINTAINING TOMORROW'S GREEN VEHICLES*

battery power alone, and some can be plugged in to recharge the battery. All hybrids use advanced technologies, such as **regenerative** braking, electric motor drive, or automatic start/shutoff, to obtain and save more energy, and to reduce fuel usage.

## *Regenerative Braking*

Unlike standard gasoline-powered cars, hybrid cars are often more fuel efficient during city driving. This is because hybrids use the frequent braking that occurs to generate and save electricity for later use by the motor.

**Did You Know?**
Ferdinand Porsche developed a hybrid car in 1900!

*The Lohner-Porsche Mixte Hybrid, shown here, was the first gasoline-electric hybrid automobile.*

CHAPTER 2: GREEN VEHICLES

*Vehicles that run on electricity alone will need special service stations like this charging station in Rio de Janeiro, Brazil. This station is especially environmentally friendly, since it is fueled by solar energy.*

## Electric Motor Drive/Assist

The electric motor gives additional power to the engine during acceleration, passing, or hill climbing. As a result, a smaller, more efficient engine can be used in a hybrid car.

## Automatic Start/Shutoff

This feature automatically shuts off the engine when the vehicle stops and restarts it when the accelerator is pressed. This prevents wasted fuel and energy as a result of idling.

## Other Green Vehicles

Electric cars, hydrogen cars, biodiesel cars, and fuel cell cars are other green vehicles that are not yet as common on the roads today. Electric cars are powered only by an electric motor and a battery. Hydrogen cars burn hydrogen, instead of gasoline, to fuel the motor. Biodiesel cars are powered using biodegradable biodiesel fuel, which is oil made from vegetables or animal fats. A fuel cell car uses a chemical reaction between hydrogen and oxygen to generate the electricity that runs the car.

## Green Mechanics

The increase in green vehicles on the roads means there will be an increase in the need for mechanics trained to work on these vehicles. Mechanics need special training to learn how to maintain and repair hybrid electric cars and the other green vehicles. Currently, most of the mechanics with this special training work for car manufacturers and dealers. However, with over a million hybrids on the road now and additional green vehicles entering the market every year, independent mechanics will need training to help meet the growing demand for service.

## If You Have a Realistic Personality...

Modern mechanics may be a good career choice for you, since it will give you plenty of opportunities for practical, hands-on work. Here are a couple of the best jobs for you. (These tables also include the average salary you can expect to earn in U.S. dollars in these jobs and how many openings are projected to exist in the United States each year for these jobs. The information comes from the U.S. Bureau of Labor Statistics.)

| JOB | ANNUAL EARNINGS | ANNUAL OPENINGS |
| --- | --- | --- |
| industrial machinery mechanics | $42,350 | 23,361 |
| mobile heavy equipment mechanics | $41,450 | 11,037 |

*Whatever is worth doing at all, is worth doing well.*

—Philip Stanhope

### ABOUT THE QUOTE

You can work just to earn a living—or you can work to achieve something that truly satisfies you as a human being. Since you're going to spend a good percentage of your adult life at work, it makes sense to find something you truly enjoy. Once you've found that, next you can choose whether you want to settle for just getting by at your job—or if instead, you want to constantly learn and become the best you can be at your job. You'll find that the things you do well, taking time to learn all you can in order to excel, are usually the things you most enjoy.

# CHAPTER 3
# EDUCATION AND TRAINING

> **WORDS TO KNOW**
> *vocational school*: A school that offers education that is focused on a certain occupation and its skills.
> *apprenticeship*: A program in which a trainee works under a skilled employer to learn a trade while working and earning wages.
> *associate degree*: The degree given to a student who completes two years of study, usually given by community colleges.
> *analytical*: Related to using logic and reasoning to think about something.

Workers in the automotive industry have a variety of educational and training backgrounds. A worker beginning right out of high school starts as a trainee. While some mechanics can learn their jobs in a few months, the more skilled jobs require years to learn and are usually learned through a combination of classroom instruction and on-the-job training.

In fact, because vehicles are becoming more computerized, and automotive maintenance and repair is becoming highly technological, employers are increasingly looking to hire trained mechanics. Technicians who have completed a formal training program in high school or in a postsecondary *vocational school* or community college will be most attractive to potential employers. Acquiring National Institute for Automotive Service Excellence (ASE) certification will also increase employment opportunities and is important for mechanics seeking work in large, urban areas.

## Vocational Training Programs

Most employers regard the successful completion of a vocational training program in automotive service technology as the best preparation for trainee positions. High school programs, while a good introduction, vary greatly in quality and scope. As a result, many graduates of these programs need further training to become qualified technicians. Exceptions to this are graduates of Automotive Youth Education Services (AYES) programs.

### AYES

Some of the more extensive high school programs participate in AYES, a partnership between high school automotive repair programs, automotive manufacturers, and franchised automotive dealers. The National Institute for Automotive Service Excellence certifies all AYES high school programs. Therefore, students who complete these programs are well prepared to enter entry-level technician positions or to advance their technical education. In addition to training in automotive repair, courses in electronics,

CHAPTER 3: EDUCATION AND TRAINING

*Apprenticeships are a great way to gain hands-on training and learn from an experienced mechanic, usually while earning some money at the same time.*

physics, chemistry, English, computers, and mathematics provide a good educational background for a career as a mechanic.

## Postsecondary Training Programs

Postsecondary automotive technician training programs usually provide intensive career preparation through a combination of classroom instruction and hands-on practice. Schools update their curriculums frequently to reflect changing technology and equipment. Some trade and technical school programs provide concentrated training for six months to a year, depending on how many hours the student attends each week, and upon completion, award a certificate.

### Community Colleges

Community colleges are an excellent postsecondary option for students interested in a career in automotive service. Community colleges are good places to learn job skills for a number of reasons. They have low tuition and an open-admissions policy, and they offer many courses, including classes that will help prepare students for the automotive industry. Community colleges are also flexible; at most community colleges, nearly 50 percent of the students work full time, so the colleges offer courses at convenient times.

Many workers choose a community college when they want to enter a new field or upgrade their skills in order to advance their career. A person with a college degree often attends a community college to update work skills. In addition, *apprenticeship* programs are increasingly linked to community college programs.

Community college programs usually award a certificate or an *associate degree*. Some students earn repair certificates in a particular skill and leave to begin their careers. Associate degree programs usually take two years to complete and include classes in English, basic mathematics, computers, and other subjects, as well as automotive repair. Recently, some programs have added classes on customer service, stress management, and other useful skills. Some formal training programs have alliances with tool manufacturers that help entry-level technicians accumulate tools during their training period.

Some car manufacturers or dealers also sponsor associate degree programs through community colleges or other postsecondary schools. Students in these programs typically alternate between full-time classroom study and working full-time in the service shops of their sponsoring manufacturer or dealer. These programs work like apprenticeships, so that when in the service shop, the student works with an experienced worker who provides hands-on instruction.

## On-the-Job Training

New mechanics usually start as trainee technicians, technicians' helpers, or lubrication workers, and gradually gain and practice their skills by working with experienced workers. In many cases, this on-the-job training is offered as part of a formal education program. With only a few months' experience, beginners can perform many routine service tasks and make simple repairs.

While some graduates of postsecondary automotive training programs often are promoted after only a few months on the job, it typically takes two to five years of experience to become a fully qualified service technician. An additional one to two years of experience familiarizes technicians with most types of repairs, but complex specialties, such as transmission repair, require another year or two of training and experience. In contrast, brake specialists may learn their jobs in considerably less time because they do not need complete knowledge of automotive repair.

Service shops and other employers often send experienced automotive service technicians to manufacturer training centers to learn how to repair new car models or to receive specialized training in the repair of certain parts, such as electronic fuel injection or air-conditioners. Dealers and other service providers may send promising beginners or experienced technicians to manufacturer-sponsored technician training programs to upgrade or maintain their skills. Factory representatives also visit service shops to give short on-site training sessions.

## Other Skills

Being a successful automotive mechanic often requires an investigative personality (see the information on personality types at the end of each chapter). The ability to diagnose the source of a malfunction quickly and accurately requires good problem-solving abilities as well as an in-depth knowledge of automobiles. Many mechanics consider diagnosing hard-to-find troubles one of their most challenging and satisfying duties. Employers look for trainees with mechanical aptitude, knowledge of how cars work, and strong communication and *analytical* skills. In addition, good reading, math, and computer skills are needed for the study of technical manuals, as well as to keep up with new technology,

## ASE-Certified Technician's Code of Ethics

1. I will strive to produce nothing but first-class workmanship.

2. I will take advantage of every opportunity to increase my knowledge/skills concerning the work I am doing. I will dedicate myself to lifelong learning.

3. I will use only those materials that are proven to be safe and recommended by the manufacturer.

4. I will recommend to an owner only that work on the vehicle which I believe to be necessary.

5. I will treat an owner's vehicle as I would my own.

6. I will attempt to correct any honest mistake made by another technician, without damaging the reputation of that person or their business.

7. I will conduct myself so as to maintain and increase the public respect for all ASE-certified technicians.

8. I will practice Service Integrity, which means that to the best of my ability I will always work for the best interest of the owner, my employer and myself.

Date_____ Signature_____

**ASE**
National Institute for
**AUTOMOTIVE SERVICE EXCELLENCE**
101 Blue Seal Drive, SE, Suite 101 • Leesburg, VA 20175 • Web: www.ase.com

*Earning a National Institute for Automotive Service Excellence (ASE) certification will increase employment opportunities and is important for mechanics seeking work in large, urban areas.*

and learn new service and repair procedures and specifications. Finally, training in electronics is very important because electrical components account for most problems in modern vehicles.

## Career Advancement and Certification

While not mandatory, ASE certification has become standard for automotive service technicians. It is not required for all automotive service technicians, but certification is common among experienced technicians in large, urban areas. Testing series and certification are available in many different areas of automotive and related services:

- automobile/light truck certification tests
- automobile service consultant test
- alternate fuels series
- medium/heavy truck test series
- truck equipment test series
- school bus test series
- transit bus test series
- collision repair and refinish test series
- damage analysis and estimating certification
- engine machinist test series
- parts specialist
- advanced engine performance specialist test
- electronic diesel engine diagnosis specialist test
- undercar specialist designation

For certification in each area, technicians must have at least two years of experience and pass an examination. Completion of an automotive training program in high school, vocational or trade school, or community or junior college may be substituted for one year of experience. To earn ASE certification as a Master Technician, you must complete seven test series and pass examinations in all. ASE certified technicians must recertify in each test area every five years to maintain their certification status.

Learning multiple auto repair services will increase a technician's value to her employer; this additional training is also likely to increase the technician's wages. Experienced technicians with administrative ability sometimes advance to shop supervisor or service manager. Mechanics who work well with customers may become automotive repair service estimators, or find work as educators. Finally, some entrepreneurial mechanics choose to open and run their own automotive repair shops.

## If You Have an Investigative Personality...

You may be happy in many modern mechanics jobs where you will have opportunities to understand and solve mechanical problems. Be aware, though, that mechanics is not about theory—it also requires the ability to repair machines with hands-on, practical work.

## If You Have an Artistic Personality...

Being a mechanic probably isn't the best career choice for you, since careers in this field will not give you enough opportunities for creativity and self-expression.

*The best preparation for good work tomorrow is to do good work today.*

—Ebert Hubbard

### ABOUT THE QUOTE

The future seldom springs up out of nowhere, taking you totally by surprise. Instead, the future will grow out of who you are right now, and today will lead you naturally into tomorrow. Whatever career interests you, begin to be involved in that today. If mechanics appeals to you, find opportunities now to take apart engines and put them back together again. Watch people who know what they're doing in an engine. Find opportunities to practice and learn. Don't be afraid to try out the first steps of a career path today. If it's not the right path for you, you'll find out now—and if it is the right one, you'll be that much further along it.

# CHAPTER 4
# JOB OPPORTUNITIES AND RELATED OCCUPATIONS

## WORDS TO KNOW
***diesel engine***: A type of internal combustion engine, in which heat produced by the compression of air in the cylinder is used to ignite the fuel; diesel also refers to the special type of fuel used in diesel engines.
***retrofit***: To replace parts with updated parts.
***longevity***: The length of life or usefulness.

## WHICH AUTOMOTIVE CAREER IS RIGHT FOR YOU?

A student or young adult interested in a career as a mechanic has many choices for his or her career path. Knowing your talents and interests ahead of time will help you make the right choices regarding education and training. In addition, knowing where the best job opportunities are and what each job does will help guide you down the best career path.

According to the Bureau of Labor Statistics, automotive service technicians and mechanics held about 723,400 jobs in 2010.

Most of these jobs were at automotive repair and maintenance shops or automobile dealers, with 31 percent working in shops and 28 percent employed by dealers. In addition, automotive parts, accessories, and tire stores employed 7 percent of automotive service technicians. Others worked in gasoline stations; automotive equipment rental and leasing companies; federal, state, and local governments; and other organizations. About 16 percent of service technicians were self-employed, compared with only 7 percent of all other installation, maintenance, and repair occupations.

## Related Occupations

### Automotive Body and Related Repairers

Automotive body and related repairers, often called collision repair technicians, straighten bent bodies, remove dents, and replace crumpled parts that cannot be fixed. They repair all types of vehicles, and although some work on large trucks, buses, or tractor-trailers, most work on cars and small trucks. They may work alone, with general direction from supervisors, or as specialists on a repair team.

Each damaged vehicle presents different challenges for repairers. Using their knowledge of automotive construction and repair techniques, automotive body repairers must decide how to handle each job based on the material from which the vehicle is made and what needs to be fixed. They must first determine the extent of the damage and decide which parts can be repaired or need to be replaced.

### Real-Life Mechanic

Chuck Glass teaches automotive technology at Bowling Green High School in Bowling Green, Kentucky. Glass is himself a graduate of a high school automotive program. After graduation, he participated in their work-study program and earned over fifteen years of experience in the automotive industry. He learned additional skills as a wheel and track vehicle mechanic in the army and by working for eight years at his father's automotive repair facility in Bowling Green as an auto technician, shop foreman, and service manager. Today he is an ASE-certified technician.

"Technical skills and knowledge can go a long way," Glass says about a career in the automotive industry.

(From www.b-g.k12.ky.us/Schools/bghs/depts/careerandtech/glass.htm)

## Diesel Service Technicians and Mechanics

Diesel service technicians and mechanics, including bus and truck mechanics and *diesel engine* specialists, repair and maintain the diesel engines that power transportation equipment. Other diesel technicians and mechanics work on other heavy vehicles and mobile equipment, including bulldozers, cranes,

# MODERN MECHANICS: MAINTAINING TOMORROW'S GREEN VEHICLES

*Jessica Koker is a mechanic with the United States Navy. The skills she learns while in the military will make her more attractive to future employers.*

CHAPTER 4: JOB OPPORTUNITIES AND RELATED OCCUPATIONS 51

road graders, farm tractors, and combines. Diesel mechanics also repair diesel-powered passenger automobiles, light trucks, or boats.

Increasingly, diesel technicians must be able to adapt to customers' needs and to new technologies. It is common for technicians to handle all kinds of repairs, working on a vehicle's electrical system one day and doing major engine repairs the next. Just as with automotive work, diesel maintenance is becoming more complex, as a growing number of electronic parts are used to control the operation of an engine. For example, microprocessors now regulate and manage fuel injection and engine timing, increasing the engine's efficiency. Also, new emissions standards may require mechanics to **retrofit** engines with emissions control systems, such as emission filters and catalysts, to comply with pollution regulations.

## Heavy Vehicle and Mobile Equipment Service Technicians and Mechanics

Heavy vehicles and mobile equipment are indispensable to many industrial activities, from construction to railroad transportation. Various types of equipment move materials, till land, lift beams, and dig earth to pave the way for development and production. Heavy vehicle and mobile equipment service technicians and mechanics repair and maintain engines and hydraulic, transmission, and electrical systems for this equipment. Farm machinery, cranes, bulldozers, and railcars are all examples of heavy vehicles that require such service.

Service technicians perform routine maintenance checks on agricultural, industrial, construction, and rail equipment. They service fuel, brake, and transmission systems to ensure peak performance, safety, and *longevity* of the equipment. Maintenance checks and comments from equipment operators usually alert technicians to problems. After locating the problem, these technicians rely on their training and experience to use the best possible technique to solve it.

## Small Engine Mechanics

Small engine mechanics repair and service power equipment ranging from jet skis to chainsaws. Mechanics usually specialize in the service and repair of one type of equipment, such as motorcycles, motorboats, and outdoor power equipment, although they may work on closely related products.

## Military Mechanics

Are you interested in a career as a mechanic, but you are thinking of going into the military first? Each branch of the military needs mechanics to maintain and repair vehicles, and the military offers training that will make a mechanic more attractive to other employers at the end of his or her military service. Each branch of the military has a large variety of mechanic positions. For example, the following list is a sample of the automotive or related mechanics careers available in the United States Army:

- construction equipment repairer
- tank system maintainer

CHAPTER 4: JOB OPPORTUNITIES AND RELATED OCCUPATIONS

- helicopter repairer
- railway equipment repairer
- watercraft engineer
- wheeled vehicle mechanic

## If You Have a Social Personality . . .

You may enjoy working in a service garage where you will have lots of contact with the customers. This type of position will give you opportunities to help people who need you, and your helpful, friendly nature will be an asset for you as you work with customers. Remember, though—being a mechanic always requires that you be able to do more than just schmooze with the customers. You must also have the skills, patience, and mechanical know-how to do the work.

*Value what you're doing. Treat it with respect. Learn everything it has to teach you. You might learn practical skills you can transfer to later work. . . . Recognize that there is something to learn from everything and determine to learn it.*

—Lawrence G. Boldt

## ABOUT THE QUOTE

When you enter the work world for the first time, you may not get the ideal job you've always dreamed of having. Very few people are that lucky. But do your best at whatever job you land—and by doing so you will learn valuable skills you'll be able to use in a better job down the road. You're also more likely to impress those around you, which could lead to new opportunities. Don't be ashamed to begin small!

# CHAPTER 5
# THE FUTURE OF MECHANICS

> **WORDS TO KNOW**
> ***marketable***: Able to be sold.
> ***recession***: A period of economic decline, where there are fewer jobs and less money.
> ***prospective***: Referring to something that is potential or possible in the future.

If you are interested in becoming a mechanic, you will need to acquire the necessary training to make yourself *marketable* to employers. Employment of automotive service technicians and mechanics is expected to increase by 17 percent between 2010 and 2020, faster than the average of 14 percent for all occupations. This will lead to new jobs for entry-level workers performing basic car maintenance and repair, such as oil changes or brake repairs. Also, vehicles are remaining in use for longer—cars last longer, and due to the effects of **recession**, car owners are keeping cars longer than in the past. These older vehicles will increase the demand for repair services, especially post-warranty work.

The increasing use of advanced technology in automobiles will also lead to new opportunities for repair technicians, especially those with specialized skills or certifications. Mechanics with expertise in certain makes or models of vehicles, or with an advanced understanding of certain systems will have an advantage over entry-level workers. In addition, an increase in the number of alternative fuel vehicles, and vehicles using hybrid-fuel technology, will raise the demand for mechanics that are trained in proper care and repair of these systems.

## Job Prospects

In addition to openings from growth, many job openings will be created by the need to replace retiring technicians. The loss of these experienced mechanics will mean the loss of a large existing knowledge base in the industry. The knowledge and experience held by these retiring mechanics was gained through many years of on-the-job experience. Entry-level trainees can never have this same level of knowledge. As a result, employers have difficulty finding workers with the right skills.

| Occupational Title | SOC Code | Employment, 2008 | Projected Employment, 2018 | Change, 2008-18 Number | Change, 2008-18 Percent |
|---|---|---|---|---|---|
| Automotive service technicians and mechanics | 49-3023 | 763,700 | 799,600 | 35,900 | 5 |

## Real-Life Green Mechanic

Luscious Garage, located in the San Francisco Bay Area, is a very unique independent mechanic shop. Run by Carolyn Coquilette, the shop is clean and green in more ways that one. First of all, Luscious is committed to reducing its own impact on the environment through the use of solar panels for energy, homemade vinegar-based window washing fluid, and carefully separated recycling containers, for everything from paper to oil. The shop itself is also known for its extreme cleanliness; one customer says, "You could eat off her floor."

Perhaps the most unique thing about Luscious is that it services only hybrid vehicles. In fact, it is one of only three or four garages in the Bay Area that specialize in hybrids. Luscious goes a step further and offers a specialty service that makes standard hybrids into plug-in hybrids. This alteration allows the cars to drive short distances using only battery power, thus saving a little more gasoline and making the green cars a little greener.

(From www.nytimes.com/2008/11/05/us/05garage.html)

Post-secondary automotive training programs and ASE certification can provide a more complete set of skills for new mechanics and therefore will increase job opportunities for these mechanics. Workers with good diagnostic and problem-solving abilities, training in electronics, and computer skills are expected to have the best opportunities.

## Planning for the Future

The information in this book is meant to be only an introduction to mechanics, to green vehicles, and to some of the career opportunities available in the automotive industry. If you think you are interested in a career as a mechanic, it is never too early to start learning your options or to begin gaining experience.

• Speak to a school guidance counselor to get advice on how to find student job opportunities in your area.

*The future of mechanics is closely tied to the future of cars and other vehicles. Mechanics will need to constantly learn to keep up with technological advances, like plug-in vehicles or whatever other advances are on the horizon.*

- A guidance counselor can also help you research community colleges, technical schools and other training opportunities in your area.

- Take any automotive classes your high school may offer, or find out if your high school offers in-depth vocational training.

- Learn about alternative fuel options and the different types of green vehicles. Any training or knowledge you can gain about the maintenance of these alternative energy vehicles will give you an advantage over other new mechanics.

Everything you do that is related to your interest in mechanics will help guide you to the specialization for which you are most suited and will strengthen you in the eyes of *prospective* schools or employers.

## If You Have an Enterprising Personality . . .

Enterprising personalities like to start up and carry out projects, especially business ventures, so if you're also interested in mechanics, you might want to one day own your own garage or service station. This would give you opportunities to lead others and be the decision-maker.

## If You Have a Conventional Personality. . .

Being a mechanic could be an excellent career choice for you. You'll have plenty of opportunities to work with machines, using precise rules in a set, orderly way. Your attention to detail will serve you well as a mechanic.

## Further Reading

Boschert, Sherry. *Plug-In Hybrids: The Cars That Will Recharge America*. Gabriola Island, B.C., Canada: New Society Publishers, 2006.

Deitche, Scott M. *Green Collar Jobs: Environmental Careers for the 21st Century*. Santa Barbara, Calif.: Praeger, 2010.

Fuhs, Allen. *Hybrid Vehicles: and the Future of Personal Transportation*. Boca Raton, Fla.: CRC Press, 2009.

Ginger, Helen. *TechCareers: Automotive Technicians*. Waco, Texas: TSTC Publishing, 2009.

Martin, Tracy. *How to Diagnose and Repair Automotive Electrical Systems*. St. Paul, Minn.: MBI Publishing Company, 2005.

Owen, Clifton E. *Today's Technician: Basic Automotive Service and Systems*. Clifton Park, N.Y.: Delmar Cengage Learning, 2010.

Popular Mechanics. *Popular Mechanics Complete Car Care Manual: Updated & Expanded*. New York, N.Y.: Hearst; Exp Upd edition, 2005.

Sobey, Ed. *A Field Guide to Automotive Technology*. Chicago, Ill.: Chicago Review Press, Inc, 2009.

## Find Out More on the Internet

Automotive Careers Today
www.autocareerstoday.org

Automotive Youth Educational Systems
www.ayes.org

CareerOneStop
www.careeronestop.org

Green Mechanical Council
www.greenmech.org

National Automotive Technicians Education Foundation
www.natef.org

National Institute for Automotive Service Excellence
www.ase.com

State Apprenticeship Programs
www.doleta.gov/oa

U.S. Department of Energy Fuel Economy Guide
www.fueleconomy.gov

## Disclaimer

The websites listed on this page were active at the time of publication. The publisher is not responsible for websites that have changed their address or discontinued operation since the date of publication. The publisher will review and update the websites upon each reprint.

## Bibliography

Barringer, Felicity. "At Specialty Garage, Making Hybrids Even Greener," www.nytimes.com/2008/11/05/us/05garage.html (12 April 2010).

Hybrid Cars. "Is Maintenance more expensive with a Hybrid?" www.hybridcars.com/cars.html#maintain (12 April 2010).

United States Army. "Careers & Jobs—Mechanics," www.goarmy.com/JobCatDetail.do?id=8 (7 April 2010).

United States Bureau of Labor Statistics. "Automotive Mechanics," www.bls.gov/k12/build02.htm (6 April 2010).

United States Bureau of Labor Statistics. "Automotive Service Technicians and Mechanics," www.bls.gov/oco/ocos181.htm (6 April 2010).

United States Department of Energy. "How Hybrids Work," www.fueleconomy.gov/feg/hybridtech.shtml (8 April 2010).

United States Department of Energy. "Why Is Fuel Economy Important?" www.fueleconomy.gov/feg/why.shtml (8 April 2010).

United States Environmental Protection Agency. "Green Vehicle Guide," www.epa.gov/greenvehicles/Index.do (8 April 2010).

United States Environmental Protection Agency. "Pollutants and Programs," www.epa.gov/otaq/transport.htm (8 April 2010).

## Index

air-conditioning technicians 17
alternative fuel 29, 56, 59
apprenticeship 37, 40, 41
automotive service technicians 12, 14, 17–19, 21
    tools 14–17

Automotive Youth Education Services (AYES) 38, 39

Bureau of Labor Statistics (BLS) 11, 19, 35, 47

collision repair technicians 48
community college 38, 40, 58

diesel service technicians 49, 51

emissions 23–29
Environmental Protection Agency (EPA) 28

global warming 23, 24
green mechanics 34
green vehicles 29–34, 58, 59
    hybrid cars 30, 32, 33

heavy vehicle and mobile equipment service technicians 51, 52

inspection 14

mechanics
    brake 17

front-end 17
    small engine 52
military mechanics 52, 53

National Institute for Automotive Service Excellence (ASE) 38, 57
    certification 42–45

on-the-job training 41, 42

personality traits 20, 35, 45, 53, 59
pollution 24–26, 28, 51

repair service estimator 9, 12

transmission technicians 18
tune-up technicians 19, 21

vocational school 37–41

## Picture Credits

Creative Commons Attribution
    Jellaluna: pg. 18
    respres: pg. 27
    sylvar: pg. 19
    TheeErin: pg. 16

Fotolia.com
    ArchMen: pg. 15
    diego cervo: pg. 46

iQoncept: pg. 22
Kabby: pg. 58
LoopAll: pg. 8
Monkey Business: pp. 39, 54
Yuri Arcurs: pg. 36

United States Department of Defense: pg. 13
    Ace Rheaume: pg. 50

To the best knowledge of the publisher, all images not specifically credited are in the public domain. If any image has been inadvertently uncredited, please notify Harding House Publishing Service, 220 Front Street, Vestal, New York 13850, so that credit can be given in future printings.

## About the Author

Malinda Miller lives and works in upstate New York. After earning a graduate degree in anthropology, she found work at a small publisher, where she enjoys the opportunity to research and write on a variety of topics.

## About the Consultant

Michael Puglisi is the director of the Department of Labor's Workforce New York One Stop Center in Binghamton, New York. He has also held several leadership positions in the International Association of Workforce Professionals (IAWP), a non-profit educational association exclusively dedicated to workforce professionals with a rich tradition and history of contributions to workforce excellence. IAWP members receive the tools and resources they need to effectively contribute to the workforce development system daily. By providing relevant education, timely and informative communication and valuable findings of pertinent research, IAWP equips its members with knowledge, information and practical tools for success. Through its network of local and regional chapters, IAWP is preparing its members for the challenges of tomorrow.

10/8/14